IS-64.a: DHS Common Operating Picture Application

By

Fema

9/20/2016

Course Objectives

This course will familiarize the learner with the controls and functions of the DHS COP application. Upon completion of this course, the learner will have a general understanding of how to leverage the DHS COP application.

Objectives: At the end of this lesson, the learner will be able to:

1. Explain the purpose and value of the DHS COP application to DHS and mission partners
2. Describe how to access the DHS COP application
3. Describe the DHS COP application's interface and data display
4. Describe how to navigate the DHS COP application's incident tools
5. Explain how to use the DHS COP application's visualization capabilities
6. View the DHS COP application to help with decision-making during disaster response and recovery phases
7. Add and modify information in the DHS COP application to help with decision-making during a disaster
8. Request a change to the DHS COP application to help with decision-making during a suspicious incidentent

Lesson 1: Overview

Lesson Overview

This lesson provides an introduction to the DHS Common Operating Picture (COP) application and capabilities, describes how to access the COP, and describes the value the COP brings to Homeland Security missions. The lesson will: describe the purpose and capabilities of the DHS COP application; identify the application's interface and basic navigation elements; and, describe the procedure for accessing and requesting help with the DHS COP application.

Objectives: At the end of this lesson, the learner will be able to:

- Describe the value the DHS COP application brings to the Homeland Security Enterprise (HSE)
- Describe how to access the DHS COP application
- Describe the DHS COP application's interface and data display

DHS COP Authorities

While there are varying definitions and use cases for a Common Operating Picture (COP), this training module focuses on the DHS COP application built initially on these authorities:

- Post-Katrina Emergency Management Reform Act of 2006
- National Response Framework, 2008
- National Response Framework, 2013
- National Incident Management System (NIMS), 2008

The DHS COP application has matured to service the entire DHS enterprise, based on mission user requirements.

Introduction to the DHS COP Application

The DHS COP application fuses and integrates situational awareness from across the enterprise to provide actionable information sharing, enhanced contextual understanding, and geospatial awareness.

When incidents happen, government and private sector leaders need to share information, make timely and informed decisions, and identify courses of action.

The COP application provides Homeland Security users a broad set of capabilities and secure access to enterprise information using role-based access controls.

How the DHS COP Application Supports the Mission

In the past, geospatial information sharing before, during, and after an incident was not streamlined. Lacking a common electronic portal for information, the process for creating and disseminating geospatial information was not clearly established or agreed upon. This resulted in duplication of effort; inefficient communication among federal, state, and local entities; and information paralysis.

The DHS COP application streamlines the communication effort, facilitating timely decision support prior to, during, or in the aftermath of a natural disaster, act of terrorism, or other man-made disaster.

Capabilities of the DHS COP Application

CAPABILITY	DESCRIPTION
Role-Based Access	User login permissions match the DHS COP application's capabilities with the user's incident information management role
Incident Management	Display and monitor incident information in a common operating picture that is available to all Homeland Security partners
RFI Tracking	Create, edit, and manage Requests for Information (RFI) from Homeland Security partners
Map Visualization	Visualize an array of information sources on a map and create user-defined views of incident information
Reporting	Access incident related reports for the Homeland Security community
Alerts	Automatically alert users when information of interest is received or new incidents are created

Mobile Application	Access DHS COP incidents and a selection of the geospatial layers on mobile devices

Incident Tools

Access incident tools from the Incident Tools menu at the top of the DHS COP interface. The Incident Tools menu allows you to:

- Toggle the Incident list on and off via the Active Incidents button
- Create an incident
- Update an incident
- Manage images
- Manage attachments
- Create an incident-specific map
- View archived incidents
- Create sub-incidents

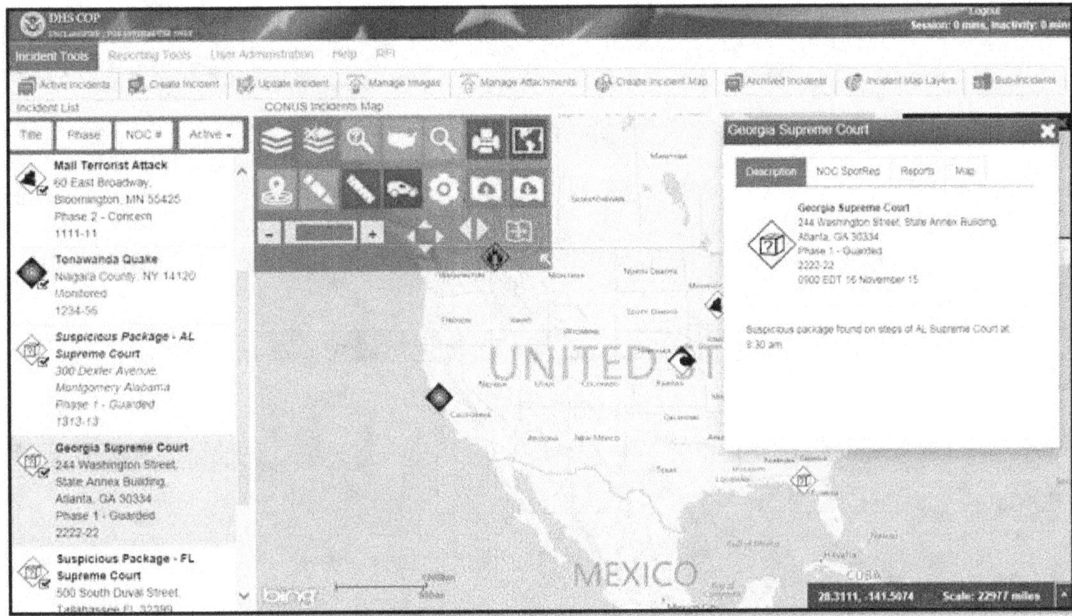

Reporting Tools

The Reporting Tools menu allows you to upload a Senior Leader Brief,
Component Report, or Media Report associated with a specific incident.

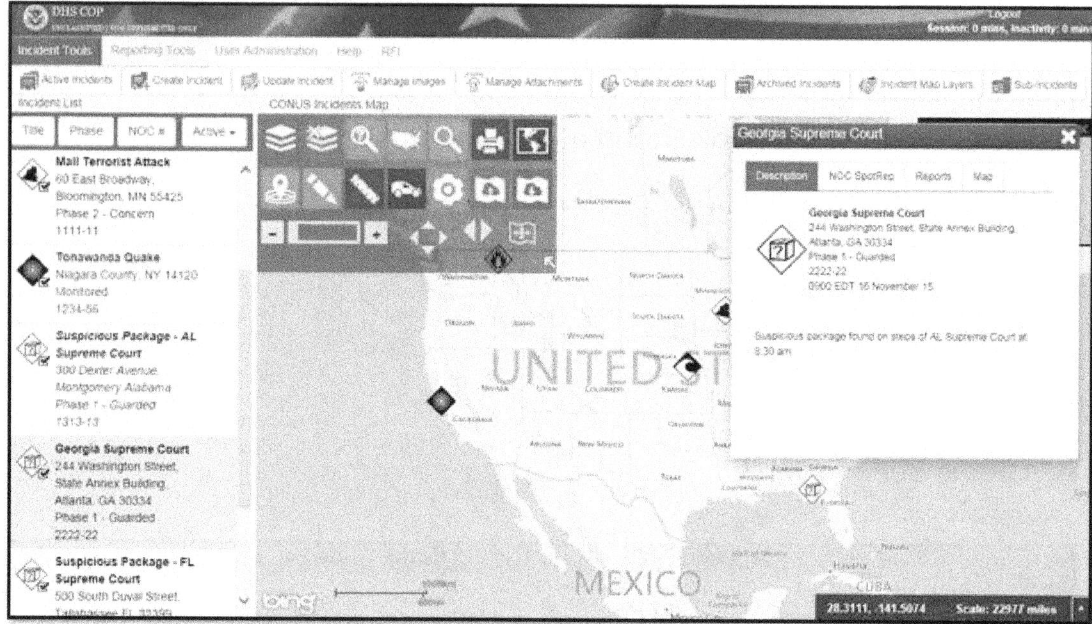

Help

The Help menu provides links to view the User Guide, Quick Reference, or
User FAQs.

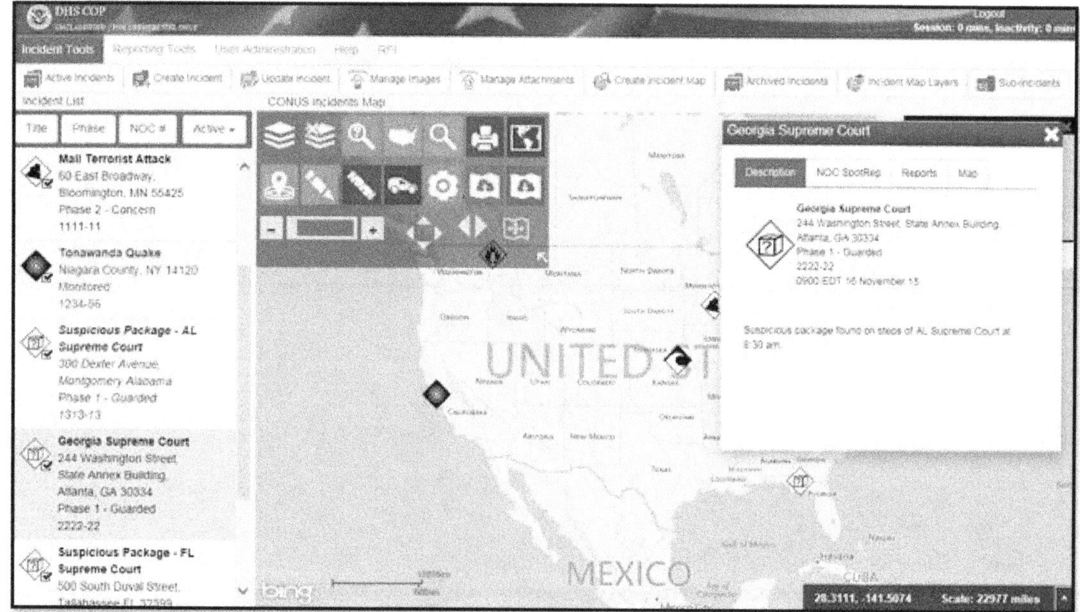

RFI

The RFI menu allows a vetted, validated member with an RFI role to log into the DHS Single Point of Service (SPS).

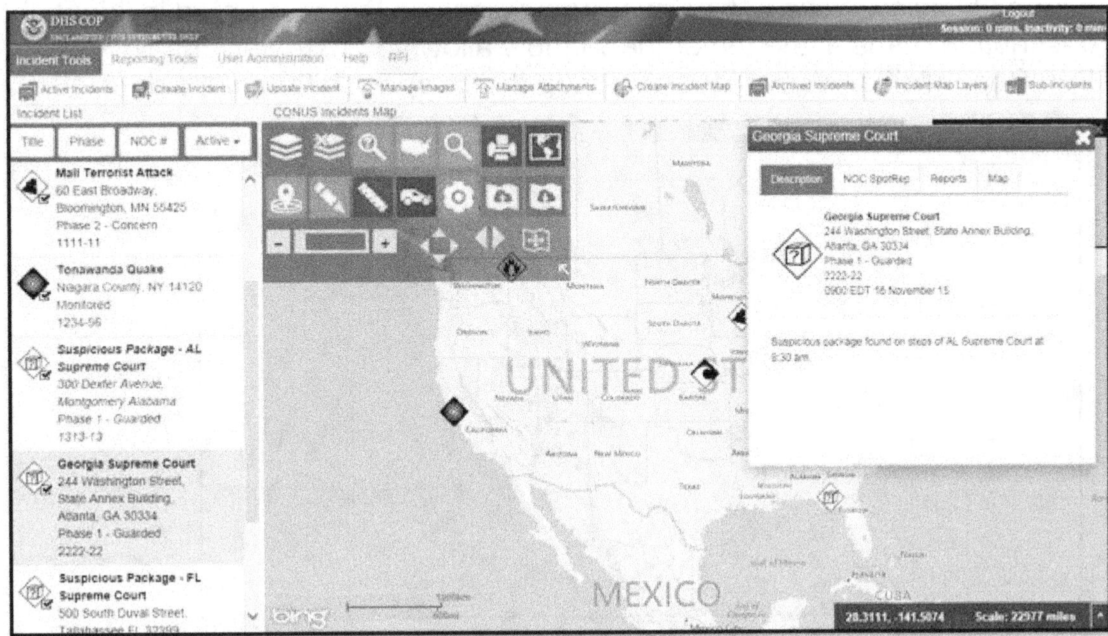

Incident List

The Incident list displays all active incidents. Four buttons at the top of the list allow you to sort the incidents by Title, Phase, National Operations Center (NOC) Number, or Active Days.

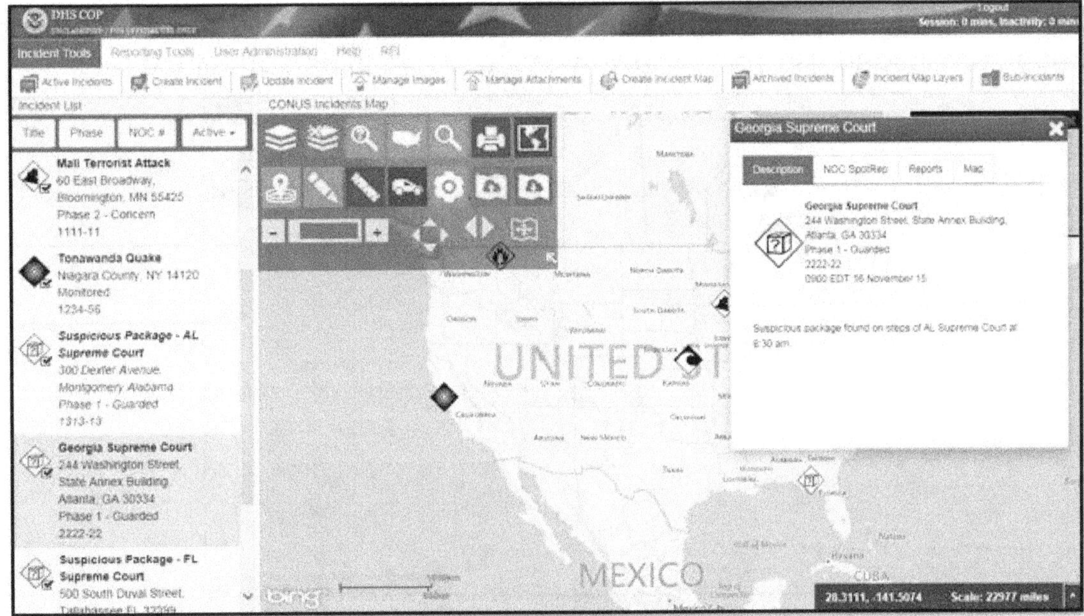

Overview Window

You can open the Overview window in two ways: select the incident name in the Incident list; or, right-click on an incident in the Incident list and select "Open Overview." The Overview window displays the associated incident description. Tabs at the top of the window allow you to review the NOC SpotRep, additional reports, and a map that is specific to that incident.

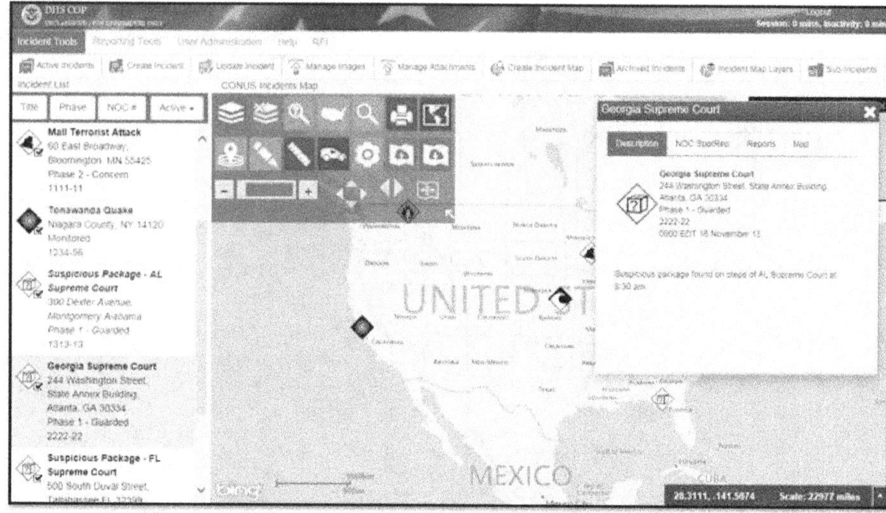

CONUS Incidents Map Area

The CONUS Incidents Map area default display includes a basemap and American National Standards Institute (ANSI) icons associated with each incident in the Incident list. Select an icon and the Overview window displays, as well as an Incident window providing a brief overview of the incident. Double-click the icon to zoom in and reposition the map. You can also click to drag the map, and use your mouse wheel to zoom in and out of the map.

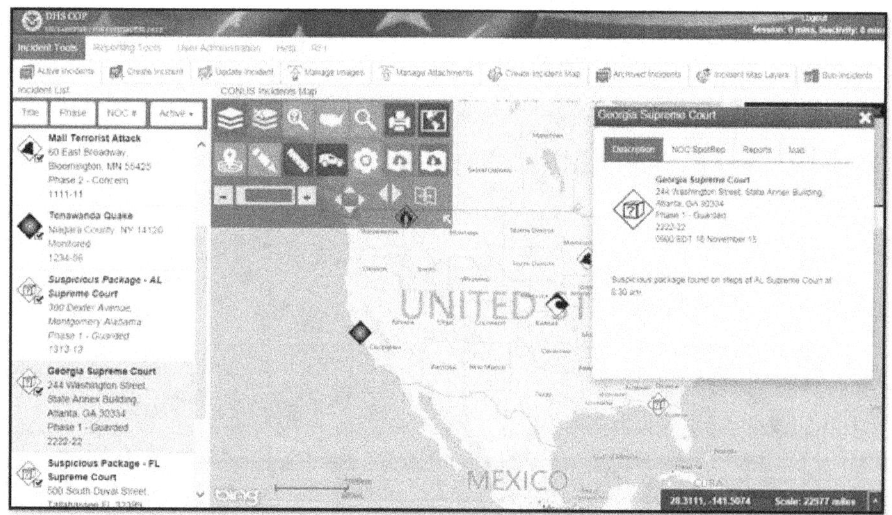

Map Toolbar

The Map toolbar allows you to: turn map layers on and off, clear all map layers, query data, zoom to CONUS, find a location, print a map, choose a basemap, find an address from a point on the map, draw, measure, get directions, set view options, save map view, and load map view. Map tools also allow you to zoom in and out of a map location, move the map in four directions, and toggle through previous map extent views. The toggle arrow in the bottom right corner of the Map toolbar allows you to hide and display the Map toolbar.

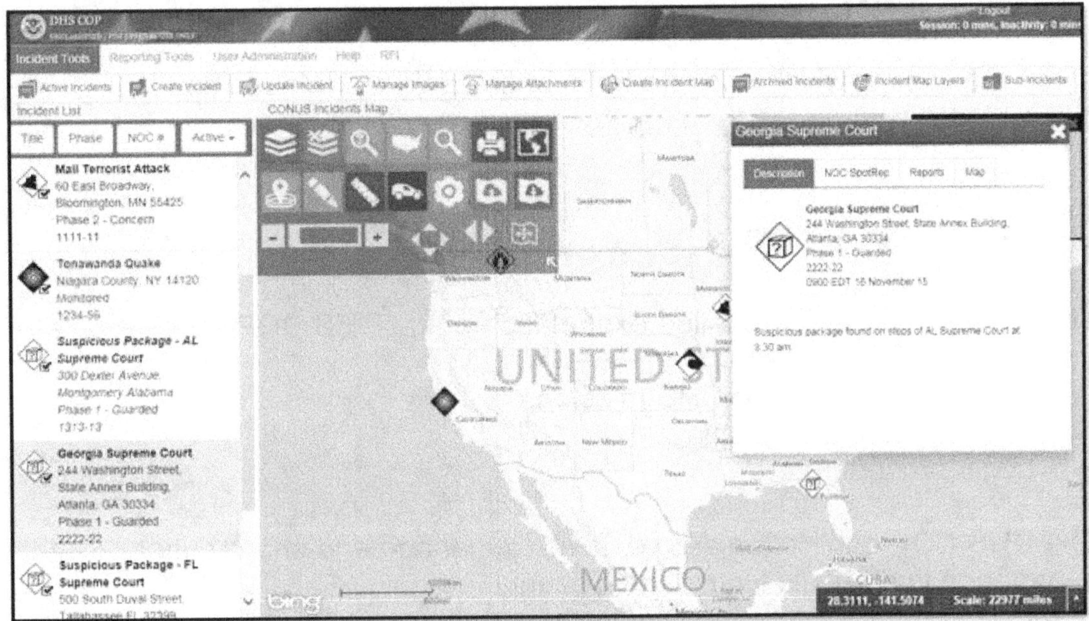

Getting Started with the DHS COP Application

To access the DHS COP application, first you must have an HSIN account. To request an HSIN account, send an email to hsin.helpdesk@dhs.gov, or call the HSIN Help Desk at 1-866-430-0162.

Once you have your HSIN account, you can request a DHS COP account by contacting the NOC via: NOC.DHSCOP.Access@hq.dhs.gov.

If you need help with the DHS COP application, call the HSIN Help Desk at 1-866-430-0162. Also, you may download the DHS COP Application User Guide from the Help menu in the COP Application.

DHS COP Application: Access-Based Controls

The DHS COP application provides access-based controls dependent upon your mission role.

Some examples include:

- Publisher
- Editor
- Administrator

If you are unsure which role you have been assigned, please contact NOC.DHSCOP.Access@hq.dhs.gov.

Lesson Summary

This lesson provided a detailed explanation of the DHS COP application's:

- Purpose and value to DHS missions
- Interface and data display
- Login procedures

The DHS COP application allows users to manage and share critical information that affects Homeland Security.

The next lesson will explore the COP in greater detail.

Lesson 2: Incident Tools

Lesson Overview

This lesson provides step-by-step demonstrations on how to navigate the DHS Common Operating Picture (COP) application incident tools. The lesson will show the learner how to access and use the Incident list, the Overview window, and the Incident Tools menu options within the COP application.

Objectives: At the end of this lesson, the learner will be able to:

- Describe how to navigate the DHS COP application's incident tools

Identifying the Status of an Incident

Each incident that appears in the DHS COP application must meet specific criteria before it is published as an active incident. To be published as an active incident, an incident must have an associated report form, image, and map created within or uploaded to the DHS COP application. Each incident is color coded to easily identify its status:

- Monitored – blue italicized text
- Published – black bold text
- Unpublished – dark blue italicized text
- Closed – purple italicized text

Sorting Incidents: A Step-by-Step Demonstration

Next, you will learn how to sort incidents by title, phase, NOC number, or the amount of days the incident has been active. This feature will help you to locate an incident quickly.

The NOC number is a unique incident number selected by the NOC analyst, or an analyst with publisher rights, for an incident.

Sorting Incidents: A Step-by-Step Demonstration - Transcript

To find an incident quickly and efficiently, you can sort the Incident List in ascending or descending order by Title, Phase, or NOC number. Note that the default sort order is by title in ascending order. Sorting is simple; just click one of the three buttons at the top of the Incident List. An arrow will appear on the button to let you know if the sort order is ascending or descending. Clicking Title for the first time selects the button, and the ascending arrow appears. Clicking "Title" a second time will change the sort order. If you need to find an incident that was active up to three days ago, click the Active drop-down list, and select 3-Day. All incidents that have been active for the past three days will display in the Incident List. The sort feature makes it easy to find an incident in the DHS COP application.

Exploring the Overview Window: A Step-by-Step Demonstration

Next, you will learn how to open and navigate the Overview window for a specific incident.

Exploring the Overview Window: A Step-by-Step Demonstration - Transcript

When you first open the DHS COP application, the default view includes the Incident List, and the CONUS Incidents Map. Clicking on an incident in the list displays the incident's details in an Overview window, and a corresponding icon highlights on the map. The Overview window has four tabs located at the top: Description, NOC SpotRep, Reports, and Map. The Description tab is the default view and provides the incident name, status, NOC number, location, phase, date, and a brief description of the incident. The NOC SpotRep tab displays the most current NOC information that has not yet been formally disseminated in a NOC report. The Reports tab includes the various reports that are available for that particular incident. The types of reports you may find in the Reports tab include: Incident Reports, Senior Leadership Briefs, Component Reports, Media Reports, and Interagency Reports and Products. Simply click on any of the available reports and that report will open in a separate window. The Map tab opens a map view of the incident location. The tools available here are identical to those on the CONUS Incident Map. However, the CONUS map includes icons and information for ALL incidents, whereas the Map tab includes information specific to only one incident.

NOC SpotRep

This tab displays the most current NOC information that has not yet been formally disseminated in an NOC report.

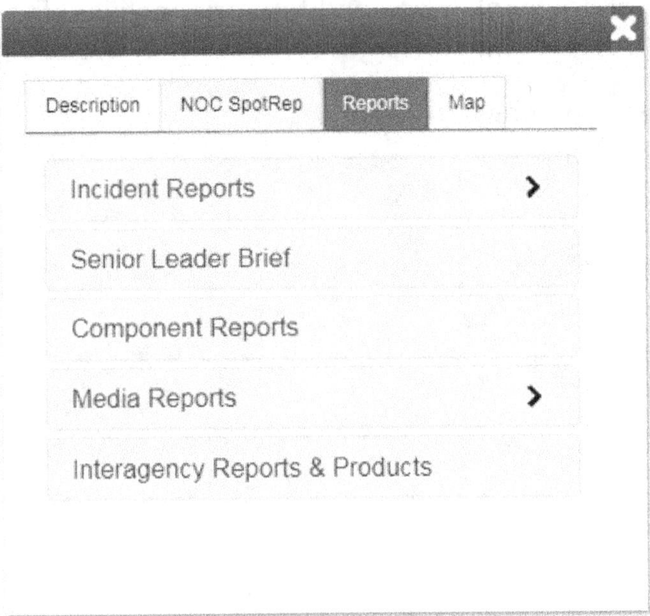

Incident Reports

This tab displays published initial and update reports released by the NOC. The incident reports appear in ascending order.

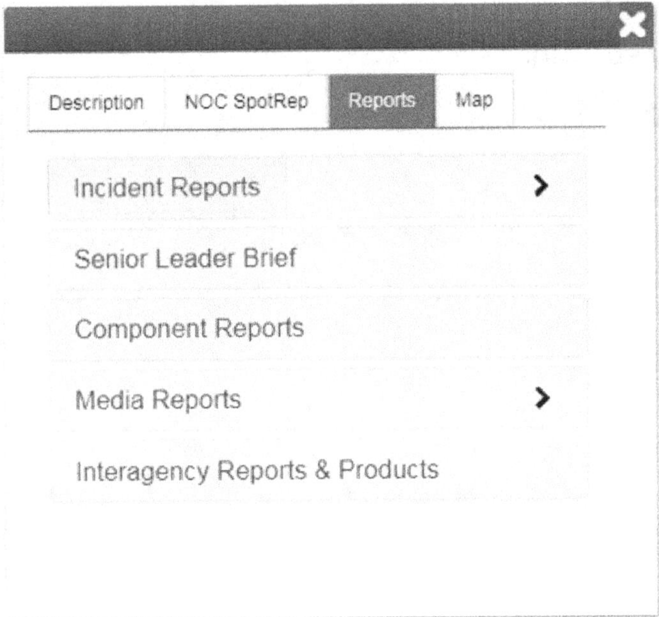

Senior Leader Brief

A Senior Leader Brief is a summary report intended for Homeland Security decision makers that provides an overview of incident information obtained from DHS components, federal, state, local, tribal, and territorial entities, the private sector, and other open-source outlets.

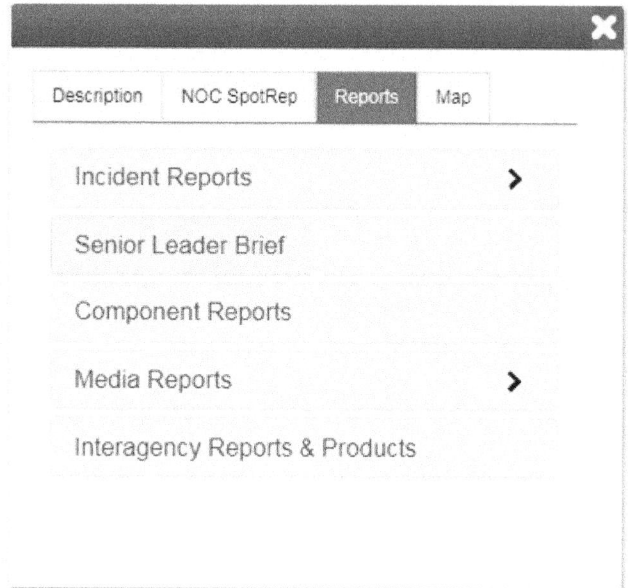

Component Reports

Component reports are comprehensive reports which provide detailed information on response activities, operational impacts, assessments, and future operations related to a specific incident.

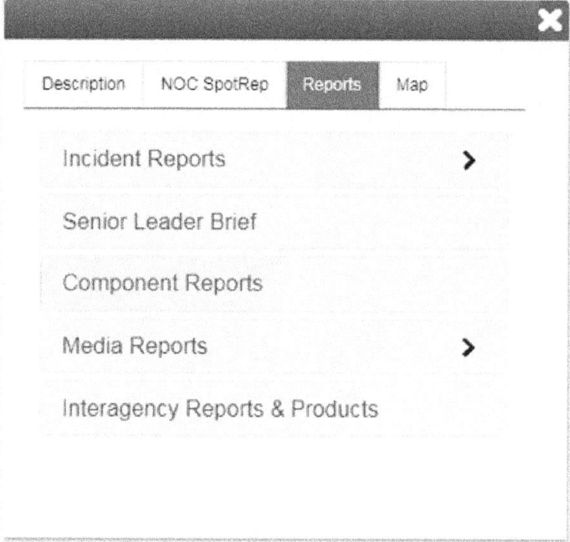

Media Reports

The Media Reports tab displays reports generated by the NOC Media Monitoring Capability. Traditional and social media monitoring provides early warning of the emerging incidents, information about continuing incidents, and issues of interest to the Homeland Security Enterprise (HSE).

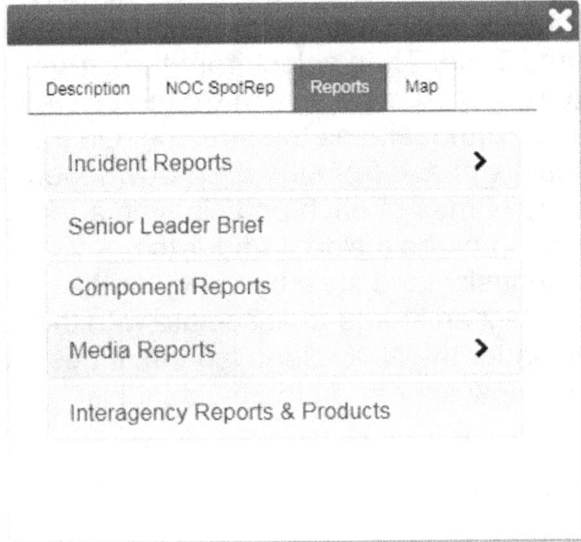

Interagency Reports & Products

This tab displays uploaded images, reports, and other digital products associated with an incident. Click any item listed in a specific folder to open it in a separate window.

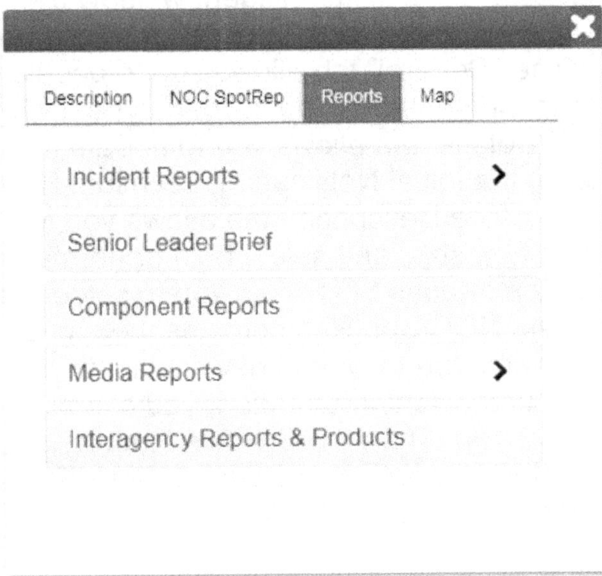

Creating a New Incident: A Step-by-Step Demonstration - Transcript

If you need to add a new incident to the Incident List, select the Incident Tools menu, then select Create Incident. A "Create New Incident" window appears. Type in the NOC Number for your incident, and provide an incident name. A new window will appear that requires additional incident information. On the General tab, provide the report Date and Time. Then select from the drop-down menus to select the incident's type and subtype. For this example, we'll select Natural Hazards as the type, and Earthquake as the subtype. On the Details tab, you must provide the incident's phase from the drop-down menu, and a location. You also must type in the names of each participating agency for the incident. Next, provide a description of the incident under the Description tab. You can change your font size and style by using the two buttons above the field. You can also select an image to associate with the incident, and include additional details under the NOC SpotRep tab, if desired. Click Save and Close. Your incident will now appear on the Incident List.

Updating an Incident Report: A Step-by-Step Demonstration - Transcript

If you need to update incident report information, simply right-click on the incident and a menu appears. From this menu, you can archive the incident, create a map for this specific incident; delete the incident; add or remove attachments and images associated with the incident; open the overview window, and update an incident. For this demonstration, we will open the Update Incident window. You can navigate the Update Incident window by using the four tabs at the top of the window, or by using the previous and next buttons at the bottom of the window. The "General" tab allows you to update the incident name, report date and time, and to select the incident type and sub-type from drop-down menus. The "Details" tab allows you to update the incident phase from a drop-down menu; the Initial Notification, Location, Report Contributors, and Participating agencies. The Description tab allows you to type information into a field, select your font size, and select bold or normal font attributes by toggling the bold button. The Images tab allows you to select the images that will be part of the report. The NOC SpotRep contains the same functionality as the description tab, allowing you to type in new incident information. Once you have updated your incident information, you can preview the report by clicking the Preview Report Tab. From the Preview Report window, you can publish the report or close the report preview window. If you publish the report, it will appear under the Reports tab/Incident Reports.

Adding an Image to an Incident: A Step-by-Step Demonstration - Transcript

When sharing information through the DHS COP application, you may want to upload a photo or graphic to include in a report. There are two ways to navigate to the Manage Images tool: You can select the Incident Tools menu, select Manage Images, and then select the specific incident; or, you can right-click on a specific incident in the Incident List, and select Manage Images. The Incident Image Management window appears. Select the "Add Image" button, and select the file you wish to upload from your computer. This image will now appear in the Update Incident window, where you can select it to add to a report.

Lesson Summary

The DHS COP application streamlines decision-making efforts and enables enterprise-wide situational awareness. This lesson demonstrated how to:

- Identify an incident's status
- Sort incidents by title, phase, NOC number, or days active
- Navigate the Overview window
- Identify the various report types available in the DHS COP application
- Create a new incident
- Update an incident report
- Add an image to an incident
- Ensure content complies with privacy laws and regulations

The next lesson will explore the COP in greater detail.

Lesson 3: Visualization Capabilities

Lesson Overview

The following lesson provides an overview of the data that is available to incorporate into the map display, and demonstrates how to: create an incident map; draw annotations on a map; measure distances on a map; add text and data layers; query a point of interest; save and load a map view; find locations, get directions, and print a map.

Objectives: At the end of this lesson, the learner will be able to:

- Explain how to use the DHS COP application's visualization capabilities

Geospatial Data Layers in the DHS COP Application

The DHS COP application accesses the rich geospatial content of the DHS Geospatial Information Infrastructure (GII), providing COP users with tremendous flexibility in the data that they can display in conjunction with the DHS COP application incident information.

The Layers window allows users to select layers from default data, to add data from defined map services, and to batch geocode a file of addresses.

Map Services Data in the DHS COP Application

Icons at the top of the Map Layers window allow you to add data from external sources to customize your DHS COP view.

To add ArcGIS Representational State Transfer (REST), Geospatial Rich Site Summary (GeoRSS), Keyhole Markup Language (KML), or Web Mapping Services (WMS), simply copy the web address into the dialog box and provide a name for the layer in the layer control.

Once added, the user can turn on/off specific layers in the REST/KML/WMS/GeoRSS under the Default Incident Layers tab.

DHS COP Application: Visualization Capabilities

To display a DHS COP layer, expand the Table of Contents list and browse to the layer you wish to view by clicking the arrows next to the item. Display a layer by checking the box next to the layer. Example layers, based upon your role, include:

Traffic Land

Traffic Land theme provides access to traffic videos throughout the U.S. It is provided by a commercial data provider and is updated in near-real time (less than one minute).

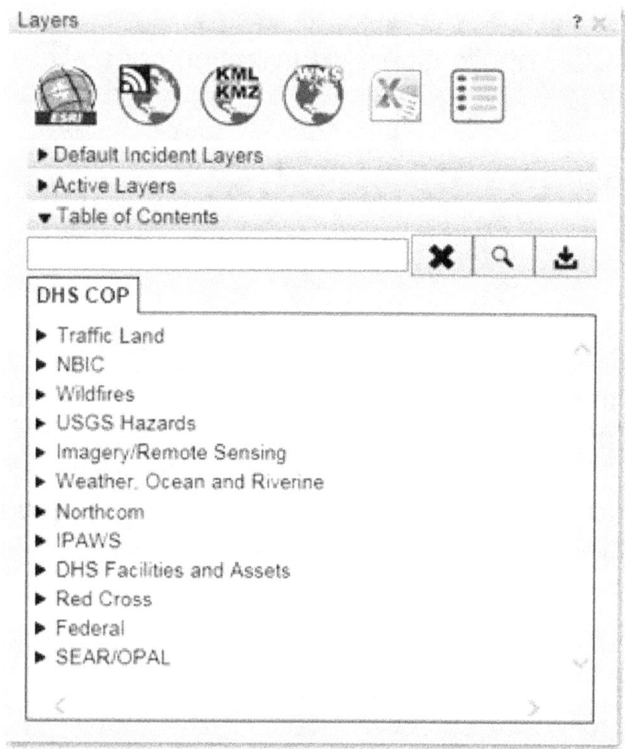

NBIC

The National Biosurveillance Integration Center (NBIC) Incident Reports theme provides current situational awareness reporting and analytical observations on emerging biological threats to the Homeland by DHS Office of Health Affairs (OHA).

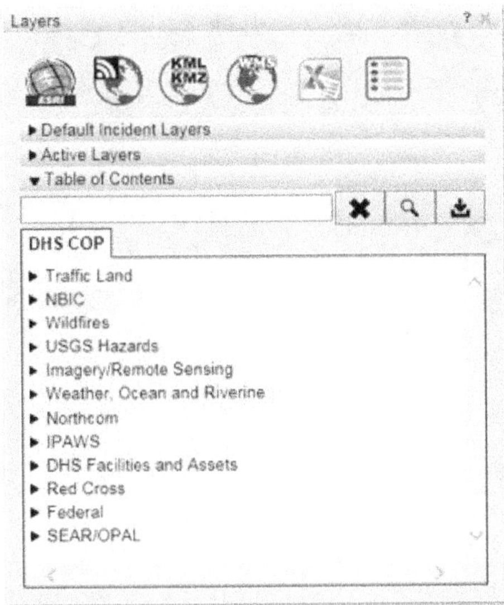

Wildfires

The Wildfires theme provides authoritative wildfire geospatial data services from the National Interagency Fire Coordination Center and the Geospatial Multi-Agency Coordination Group (GeoMAC). The layers are updated based on emerging wildfire hazards.

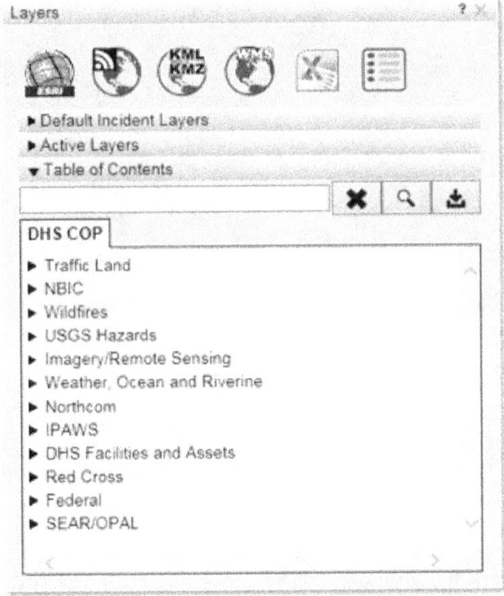

USGS Hazards

The USGS Hazards theme provides approximate locations of natural hazards such as earthquakes, wildfires, volcano activity, and floods. It is maintained by the United States Geological Survey and is updated as hazards occur in near-real time.

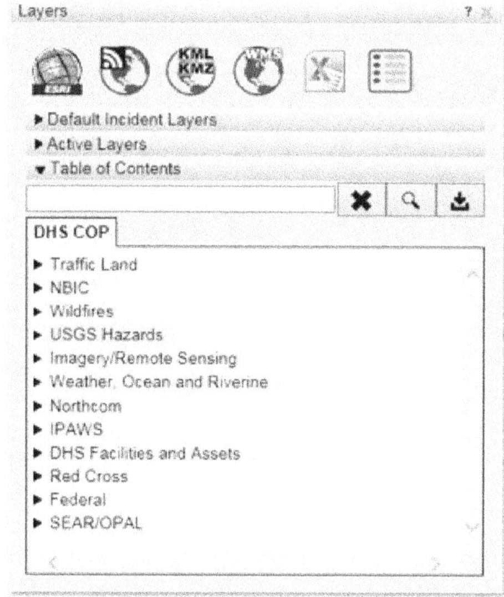

Imagery/Remote Sensing

The Imagery/Remote Sensing theme provides access to high resolution pre- and post-incident aerial and satellite imagery. It is maintained by the DHS Geospatial Management Office (GMO) and is updated based on available and emerging imagery data sources.

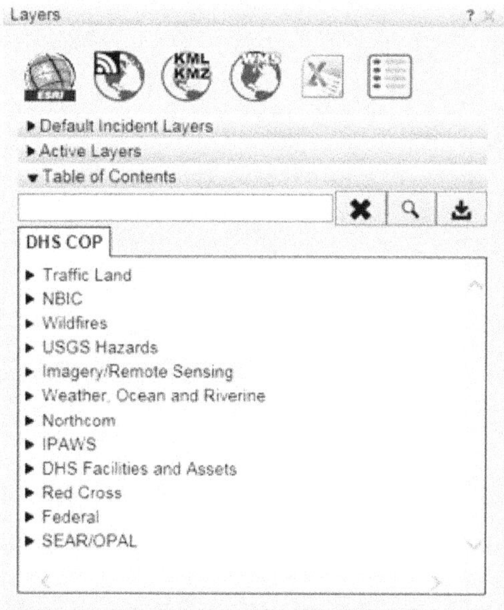

Weather, Ocean, and Riverine

The Weather, Ocean, and Riverine data layers include:

- NOAA weather watches, warnings and advisories for tornadoes, extreme weather, flooding, marine advisories and multiple data sources for tropical storms and hurricanes
- NOAA near-real-time data feeds, including infrared and visible channels from the NOAA GOES geostationary weather satellites, the National Weather Service National Radar Mosaic, and National Wind Speed and Direction
- FEMA Flood Boundaries, including the 100 and 500 year flood plains and USGS Stream Gauge information

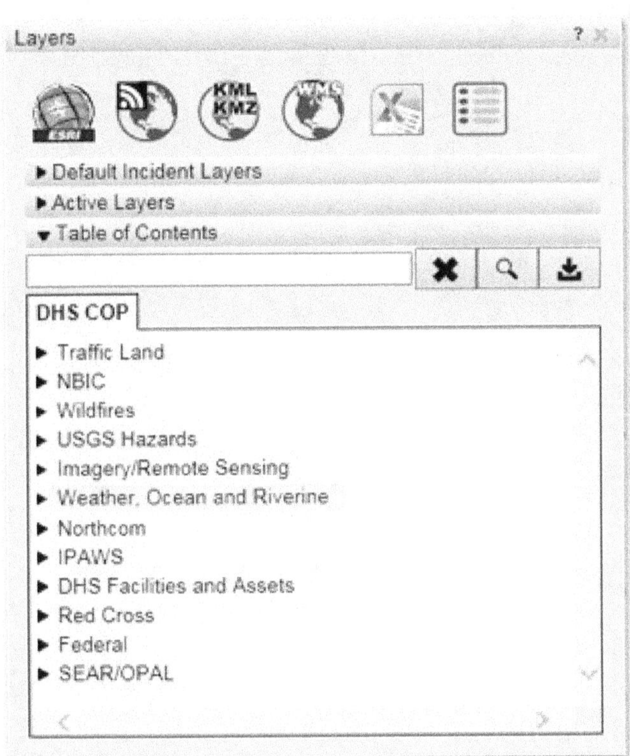

NORTHCOM

The U.S. Northern Command (USNORTHCOM) theme provides geospatial data on military asset locations such as Friendly Force Tracks and Temporary Flight Restrictions from the Federal Aviation Administration. It is provided by USNORTHCOM Situational Awareness Geospatial Enterprise (SAGE) and is updated daily.

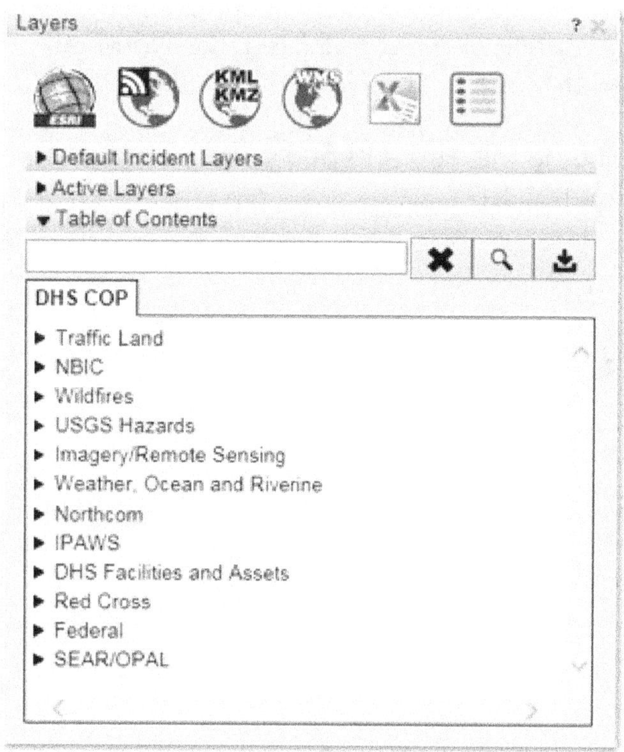

IPAWS

The Integrated Public Alert & Warning System (IPAWS) theme provides geospatial alerts and warnings originating from the Emergency Alert System, Wireless Emergency Alerts, and other federal, state, local, and tribal alerting systems. The data is administered by FEMA but is published geospatially by the GMO. It is updated in near-real time.

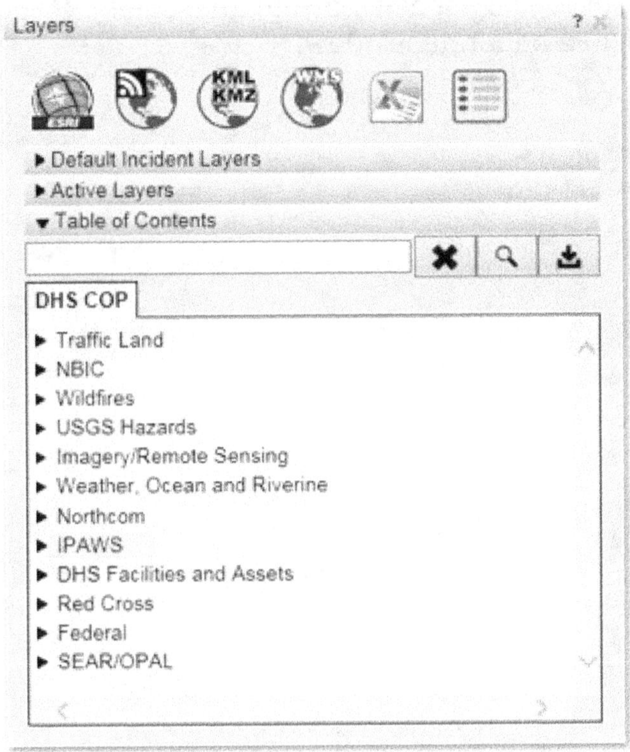

DHS Facilities and Assets

The DHS Facilities and Assets data layers include U.S. Customs and Border Protection, the U.S. Coast Guard, FEMA, the Federal Law Enforcement Training Center (FLETC), U.S. Immigration and Customs Enforcement (ICE), the Transportation Security Administration (TSA), U.S. Citizen and Immigration Service (USCIS) and the U.S. Secret Service (USSS). This area displays images, reports, and other digital products associated with an incident. Double-click any item in the list to open it in a separate window.

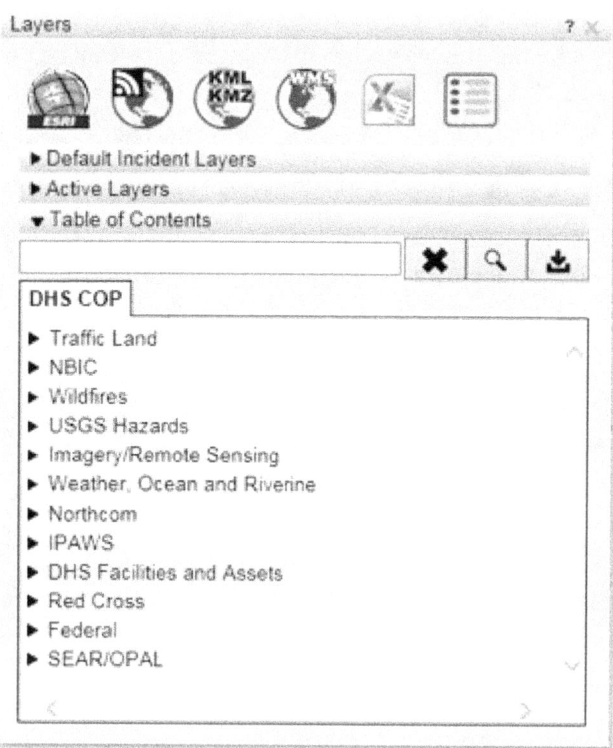

Red Cross

The Red Cross theme provides geospatial data on shelter locations and available capacity from the National Shelter System (NSS). It is administered by the American Red Cross and published geospatially by FEMA.

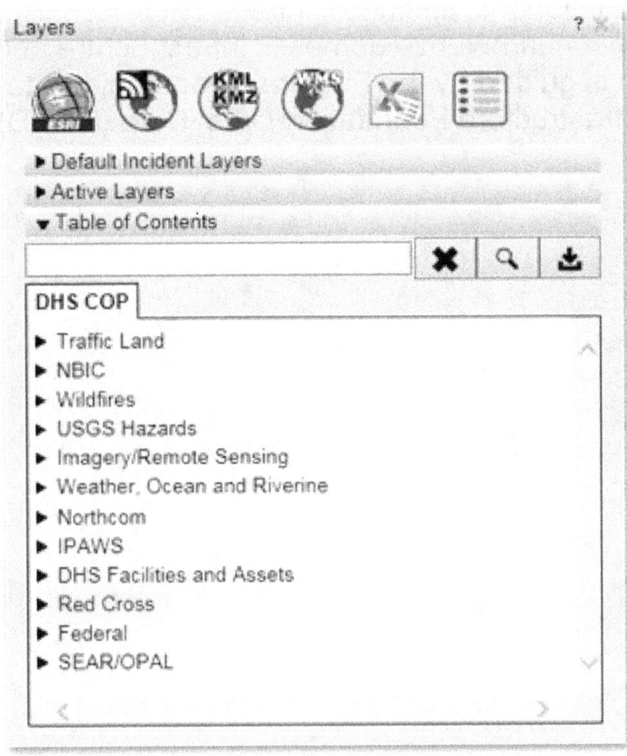

Federal

Federal foundational-level critical infrastructure content is compiled by the National Geospatial-Intelligence Agency (NGA), in partnership with the Department of Homeland Security (DHS), to support homeland security enterprise missions. Federal foundational-level critical infrastructure consists of over 550 geospatial data layers that characterize domestic infrastructure and base map features. This program is guided by the Federal Geographic Data Committee (FGDC) Homeland Infrastructure Foundation-Level Data (HIFLD) Subcommittee.

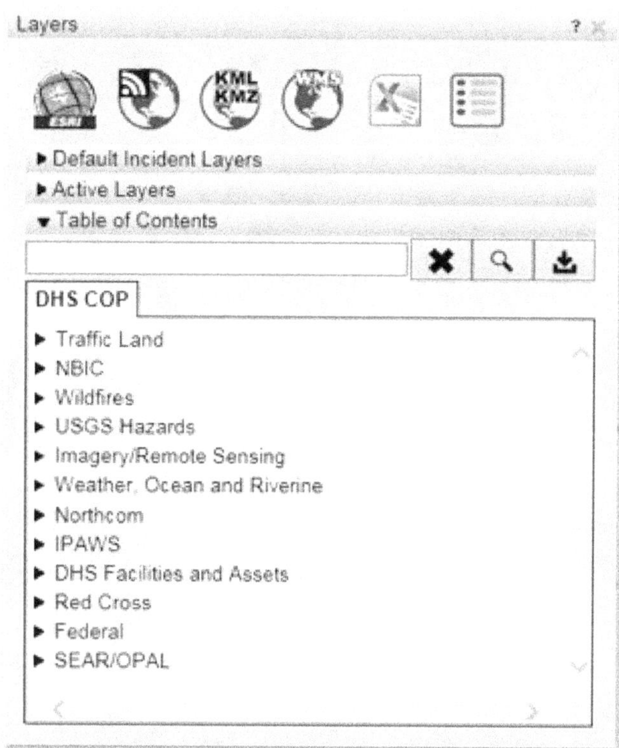

SEAR/OPAL

The Special Event Assessment Rating (SEAR) and Overseas Personnel Activity Locator (OPAL) themes provide DHS specific and sensitive geospatial data. It is maintained by the DHS Office of Operations Coordination and Planning and geospatially published by the GMO.

SEAR identifies all national, regional, state, and local events. It is updated annually.

OPAL identifies the location of all DHS personnel and activities around the world. It is updated monthly.

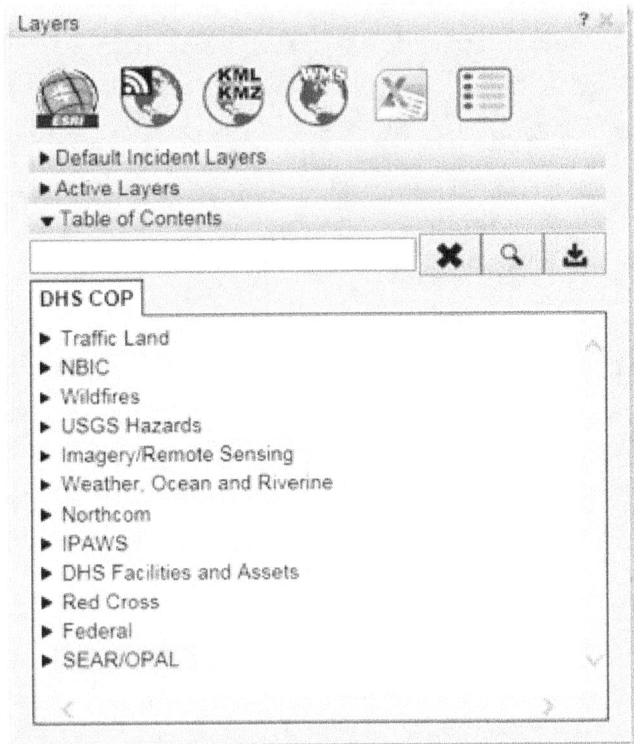

Creating an Incident Map: A Step-by-Step Demonstration

The DHS COP application provides basemap and map layering tools to add content from the GII or from external sources. Adding data layers adds incident-specific relevance to the map display.

Creating an Incident Map: A Step-by-Step Demonstration - Transcript

To build your map, begin by selecting the Incident Tools menu, and then "Create Incident Map." A window appears for you to select the incident for the map you are about to create. A new map window opens. Click the location of the incident. An icon appears in the incident location. Select the arrow in the top left side of the map to open the map toolbar. Click on the "Choose Basemap" icon to select from four available basemaps: Digital Globe, Aerial, Aerial with Labels, or Road. The default basemap is "Road." For this example, let's select "Aerial." Now, let's add layers to the basemap. The "Layers" tool allows you to add pre-populated data as a layer to your map. Start by selecting the "Map Layers" icon on the map toolbar. You will see the Layers dialog box display. Select "Table of Contents." Then, expand the Federal menu by selecting the down arrow next to Federal. Next, expand the Emergency Services menu, and then select the check box next to Receiving Hospitals. Icons will appear on the map for each Receiving hospital in your map view. If you want to delete this layer, then un-check the check box.

Drawing Lines and Polygons on a Map: A Step-by-Step Demonstration

The DHS COP application provides tools for drawing lines and shapes on the map. This feature is helpful for highlighting affected areas, routes, and other important features.

Drawing Lines and Polygons on a Map: A Step-by-Step Demonstration - Transcript

On the CONUS map, you will see a toolbar that contains the following icons: Map Layers, Clear Layers, Query Data, Zoom to CONUS, Find Location, Print Map, Choose Basemap, Address from Point, Draw, Measure, Directions, Options, Save Map View, and Load Map View. To create annotations on the map, select the "Draw" icon on the map toolbar. This opens the "Draw" window which contains the following icons: free draw, draw lines, draw shapes, apply a pin, add text, edit shapes, and erase shape.

Next, select the type of tool that you want to use to draw on the map. For this example, we'll select the "draw shapes" icon. Click on the desired area of the map and create your shape. Single click and move your cursor to define the shape. Double-click to place the final point. If you are using the line tool, click once to set the starting point of the line, the click again to draw line segments. Double-click to complete the line. If you make a mistake and want to delete your shape or line, select the eraser icon click once on the shape to erase it. To clear all shapes on the map, select the "Clear All" button."

Measuring Distances on a Map: A Step-by-Step Demonstration

The DHS COP application provides tools to measure lines and shapes on the map. This feature is helpful for calculating areas and distances within an affected area.

Measuring Distances on a Map: A Step-by-Step Demonstration - Transcript

To measure distances on a map, select the "Measure" icon on the map toolbar. From the "Measure" window, you can measure distance with one or more line segments, measure distance and area with a polygon, or measure a circular area with the radius tool. For this example, we will select the polygon icon and define an area to measure on the map. To close a polygon, simply double click. You will notice that the area and total distance appears in the Measure window. The units of measure default to Miles and Square Feet. To change the total distance unit, select a different unit from the top drop-down menu. To change the area unit, select from the bottom drop down menu. You can only measure one thing at a time, so if you start new measurement, the previous one will automatically delete. When you are finished measuring, you can delete your shape by selecting the "Clear" button.

Adding Text to a Map: A Step-by-Step Demonstration

The DHS COP application provides tools to add text annotations to a map.

Adding Text to a Map: A Step-by-Step Demonstration - Transcript

To add text annotations to a map, start by selecting the "Draw" icon from the map toolbar. The Draw window opens. Select the Add Text icon and enter desired text. Choose the font, size, color, and style; and then click on the map where you want to place the text. If you want to delete the text, select the "Clear All" button on the Draw window.

Querying a Feature: A Step-by-Step Demonstration

The DHS COP application provides a Query Data tool that allows the user to specify an area and to export the data within that defined area.

Querying a Feature: A Step-by-Step Demonstration - Transcript

Before we demonstrate the query tool, we need to add a data layer to the map so that we have some information to query. Let's imagine that a hurricane is heading toward the Pensacola, Florida area; and we need to know the location and number of public schools in that area. Public schools are listed in the Layers window under Federal, and then Education. So let's zoom in the map to the Pensacola area, and then open the public schools layer. By clicking the query tool, you will be presented a new dialogue window for query data. You may query this data layer using either the rectangular area tool, the polygon tool, or the circular area tool. For this example, let's draw a rectangle around our area of interest. Click and drag on the area that you want to query. This may take some time. The results from the query are displayed in a table which can be exported. If you want to export the results, simply select the Export button, and select from the menu of export options. A "Save as" window will display for you to provide a file name and location for the exported data. By clicking the "Query" tool, you will be presented a new dialogue tool for query data.

Save and Load a Map View: A Step-by-Step Demonstration

The DHS COP application provides features that allow you to save a map view so that you can load it later without having to rebuild it.

Save and Load a Map View: A Step-by-Step Demonstration - Transcript

When working within the CONUS Incident Map, you can use the Save Map View and Load Map View features to streamline your work flow. Once you build a map view that you want to save, select the Save Map View icon from the map toolbar. The Save Current Map View window appears. Name the map view and provide a brief description. Select the OK button. Now, select the Load Map View icon. The Saved Maps window appears; scroll down the list and you will see your saved map at the bottom. This map will be available at any time when you access the DHS COP application. To delete the map, simply click the red "x" next to the map view.

Finding Locations on a Map: A Step-by-Step Demonstration

The DHS COP application provides two ways to find locations on a map: Address from Point, and Find Locations.

Finding Locations on a Map: A Step-by-Step Demonstration - Transcript

If you need to find a location on a map, the DHS COP application provides two tools to help you: Find Location, and Address from Point. Let's explore these two tools. On the map toolbar, select the Find Location icon. A Find Location window appears. Enter the street address, city, state, and zip code, or enter a general location to search. For example, if you know the intersection, enter the street names and the city name in the location field. Then select Find Location. If you searched by general location, the map will zoom to the first location found. If multiple locations are found, they are shown in the drop-down menu. If you are searching for an address and do not know any surrounding street names, use the Address from Point tool. When the Address from Point window opens, select a point on the map. The results will display the latitude/longitude coordinates, the street address, city, state, and Zip code. If there is no address available at the point on the map, you will get a message "No address could be found for the specified location." You can copy the latitude/longitude coordinates, and the address onto your computer clipboard to paste into another software application. To clear results, select the "Clear" button.

Getting Directions and Printing a Map: A Step-by-Step Demonstration

The DHS COP application provides a Directions feature that allows the user to get directions by entering the starting and ending addresses. This feature allows point-and-click referencing on the map if actual street addresses are not available.

Results can be displayed for driving or walking, by time or by distance. Once you determine your route, you can also print the map using the Print feature.

Getting Directions and Printing a Map: A Step-by-Step Demonstration - Transcript

In an emergency situation, you may need to determine an alternate route for emergency services if roadways are blocked or damaged. The DHS COP application has a Directions tool on the Map Toolbar. To get directions, select the Directions icon. A Directions window appears. Enter the starting address by either typing in the street address, or – if you do not know the address or no address is available – simply click the index finger icon next to the Enter Starting Address field, and click the starting point on the map. Then follow the same process for entering the ending address. Select from the options to display the route by driving or walking; by time or by distance. Then select Get Route. The results appear in the directions box below. You may copy the directions to paste into another software application on your computer, and you can also print the map. To print the map, select the Print Map icon, provide a title for the map, select portrait or landscape, and select the format. Then select the Print button.

Lesson Summary

The DHS COP application provides a common source for viewing incidents on a map, adding operationally relevant mission information, and sharing the map among DHS partners. This module provided information on the various data layers available in the DHS COP application, and demonstrations for:

- Creating an incident map
- Drawing and measuring annotations on the map
- Adding text and data layers to the map
- Querying a point of interest on the map
- Saving and loading a map view
- Finding locations from a point on the map or from an address
- Getting directions and printing a map

The next lesson will explore the COP in greater detail.

Lesson 4: DHS COP Scenario for Decision Makers

Lesson Overview

This lesson will provide a use-case scenario for a decision maker during the response and recovery phases of a natural disaster. The decision maker will access the DHS COP application to view and monitor events as they occur to support situational awareness and decision making. This scenario demonstrates a "view only" access role in the DHS COP application.

Objective: At the end of this lesson, the learner will be able to:

- View the DHS COP application to help with decision-making during disaster response and recovery phases

How Decision Makers Can Use the DHS COP Application

The following scenario provides an example of how decision makers can use the DHS COP application to view and monitor events as they occur to support situational awareness and decision making during the response and recovery phases of a catastrophic earthquake.

This scenario demonstrates how to access the DHS COP application to:

- Help with decision making during an initial disaster response
- Support information sharing during search and rescue missions
- Coordinate recovery efforts in the aftermath of a disaster

DHS COP Supports Decision Making During the Initial Response to a Disaster

The initial response phase is typically the period of greatest uncertainty due to the lack of information from the field and the large number of questions and requests for information. During this phase, decision makers need to gather up-to-the-minute information to make timely and accurate evaluations.

The DHS COP application provides data to help decision makers determine how and when to deploy resources that are needed to support the initial response to a disaster.

San Francisco Earthquake Scenario: Initial Response Phase

SCENARIO: On Monday, July 27, a 7.5 magnitude earthquake hits the San Francisco bay area at 5:34 a.m. The Golden Gate and Bay bridges are impassable.

Decision makers in charge of the immediate response to this disaster can view the COP application to gain situational awareness regarding the location of electric and gas lines, commercial and government buildings, public transportation systems, and potential toxic hazards within the area of impact.

San Francisco Earthquake Scenario: Initial Response Phase - Transcript

The DHS COP application allows decision makers to view important information that contributors from the emergency response community have created to provide situational awareness for everyone involved in the response effort. For example, the identification of event damage boundaries – as shown in the incident report – helps managers to understand the operational magnitude of the event. Decision makers can view data layers within the area of impact which show the location of vital infrastructure such as: oil and natural gas pipelines, electricity transmissions lines, locations of commercial and government facilities, locations of public transportation systems, and potential toxic hazards.

San Francisco Earthquake Scenario: Lifesaving Phase

SCENARIO UPDATE: Mass casualties from the initial earthquake now stand at 2,500 and are rising. Thousands are without food, water, or shelter. Aftershocks are complicating search and rescue efforts.

During the lifesaving phase, decision makers need information to help them determine shelter availability for victims displaced by the earthquake, accessible transportation routes to the impacted area for delivery of water and blankets, and location of local medical emergency services.

DHS COP Enables Information Sharing During Lifesaving Missions

A coordinated response to an incident of this size and impact is necessary in order to save lives and to provide aid and shelter to survivors. The DHS COP application's information sharing capability supports lifesaving missions, including:

- Search and rescue efforts
- Critical medical support
- Coordination of food, shelter, and water for victims

Many of these activities are high-profile in the eyes of government officials, emergency managers, the media, and the public.

San Francisco Earthquake Scenario: Lifesaving Phase - Transcript

The DHS COP application supports decision makers as they determine missions related to life saving, medical support, shelter, and the delivery of food and water. For example, decision makers can use the DHS COP application to help identify shelter availability via the Red Cross National Shelter System data layers,and evacuation routes via the Federal Transportation Ground and Water data layers. Transportation data layers can help decision makers to determine how to deploy search and rescue teams if usual transportation routes are blocked or destroyed. Additionally, decision makers can locate surrounding emergency medical facilities by accessing the Federal Emergency Services data layer.

DHS COP Supports Recovery Missions After a Disaster

The recovery phase focuses on providing much needed assistance to communities affected by disaster events, allowing citizens to recuperate as quickly as possible.

During the recovery phase, decision makers manage and prioritize the timely restoration of damaged transportation, water, sewer, and power infrastructure; and organize temporary housing for victims.

The DHS COP application, with its numerous data layers and relevant incident reports, provides decision makers with needed information to support these efforts.

Lesson Summary

This module provided a case scenario for decision makers during the response and recovery phases of a natural disaster.

Decision makers can use the DHS COP application to view and monitor events as they occur, enhancing situational awareness. Decision makers can access the DHS COP application to support:

- Decision making during the initial response to a disaster
- Information sharing during search and rescue missions in the aftermath of a disaster
- Coordinated recovery efforts in the aftermath of a disaster

The next lesson will explore the COP in greater detail.

Lesson 5: Editing and Publishing Information in the DHS COP

Lesson Overview

This scenario demonstrates the process of editing and contributing information to the DHS COP application, based on user access. In this scenario, the user logs in as a publisher, which means he or she can add, publish, and modify information in the DHS COP application.

This scenario demonstrates how to: create a new incident in the DHS COP application to support decision makers in response to a disaster; create an incident map associated with a disaster; publish the initial report associated with a disaster; and, add map layers associated with a disaster.

Objective: At the end of this lesson, the learner will be able to:

- Add and modify information in the DHS COP application to help with decision-making during a disaster

Terrorist Attack Scenario: Creating a New Incident in the DHS COP

SCENARIO: On Saturday, December 2, at 12:30 p.m., an unknown terrorist group launched a multi-pronged attack at a major mall, using vehicle bombs, suicide bombers, and improvised explosive devices (IEDs).

Immediate reports claim approximately 75 deaths and hundreds of people injured. Details are still unfolding at the scene.

Terrorist Attack Scenario: Creating a New Incident in the DHS COP - Transcript

In response to a terrorist attack at a major mall, the publisher must create a new incident in the DHS COP application so that information can be shared across the emergency response community. To do this, select the Incident Tools menu and select "Create Incident." A "Create New Incident" window appears. Next, type in the NOC Number and the incident name, and then select "Create."

A new window opens that requires additional incident information. On the General tab, provide the report Date and Time, and then select from the drop-down menus to indicate the incident's type and subtype. For this example, select "Security" as the type, and "Terror Incident" as the subtype. On the Details tab, select the incident's phase from the drop-down menu, and a location. Then type in the names of each participating agency for the incident, and provide a description of the incident under the Description tab. Finally, click "Save" and "Close". Reload the page to update the view … the terror incident now appears in the Incident List.

Adding an Incident Map to the DHS COP

The map visualization tools within the DHS COP application can help emergency response personnel to gain situational awareness as new details become available.

Data layers pertinent to this incident may include specific damage locations to the mall infrastructure, locations of power and water supplies, locations of nearby medical facilities, first responders, and police departments.

Next, the publisher needs to create a meaningful map to closely track the challenging issues associated with this attack.

Terrorist Attack Scenario: Creating an Incident Map

SCENARIO UPDATE: Damage from large truck bombs destroyed mall access points, and timed explosive devices were detonated along the major mall exits. Additional explosions occurred outside the mall, impeding access to emergency vehicles.

Terrorist Attack Scenario: Creating an Incident Map - Transcript

Next, the publisher needs to create an incident map specific to this disaster. To do so, select the "Create Incident Map" tab on the "Incident Tools" menu bar. A "Select Incident" window appears. Select the Mall Terrorist Attack incident and click the "OK" button.

A new map window appears to identify the location of the incident. To specify
the most accurate location, use the "Find Location" feature on the map toolbar,
and type in the address for the mall, then select "Find Location." When the
location displays, click on the location and an ANSI icon appears for the
associated event type. Select "Save" and "Close."

To view map data layers that may be helpful in this scenario, zoom in to the
area of concern, and select the "Layers" icon. To see nearby emergency
services and medical facilities, select Federal, and then Emergency Services.
For example, turn on layers for Receiving Hospitals, Fire Stations, and
Emergency Medical Services; you will see icons appear on the map. Clicking
on each icon opens a dialog box that provides address and telephone
information for each facility, and a "zoom to" link that will enlarge the map view
to the facility's exact location.

Terrorist Attack Scenario: Publishing an Incident Report

SCENARIO UPDATE: Despite the limited area of impact, transportation
disruptions are spreading to a much larger area, impacting the ability of first
responders to provide support to the victims.

Publishing Information the DHS COP

During a no-notice event such as this, geospatial information arrives quickly
from a variety of sources. As the event unfolds, new information becomes
available and the publisher must be prepared to update the DHS COP
application to reflect the most timely information.

Next, the publisher must publish an Incident Report to the DHS COP
application.

Terrorist Attack Scenario: Publishing an Incident Report - Transcript

An Incident Report is released by the National Operations Center. In this
scenario, the publisher must upload new information from the Incident Report -
along with a new photograph - to the DHS COP application. To do this, right-

click on the Mall Terrorist Attack incident and select "Manage Images." Select
the "Add Image" button, browse to the new image, add a description, select
"Save Changes", and then close the window.

Next, right-click on the Mall Terrorist Attack incident and select "Update
Incident." Select the "Images" tab and click on the new image to include it in
the Incident Report, select the Description tab, copy and paste the most current
incident information from the NOC report, and then select Save. Next, select
the Preview Report button. After reviewing the report, select "Publish Report."
The report now appears in the Incident Reports section of the Reports tab in
the Overview window.

Lesson Summary

This module provided a case scenario for DHS COP application publishers in
the aftermath of a man-made disaster. This scenario demonstrated how to:

- Create a new incident in the DHS COP application to support decision
  makers in the wake of a disaster
- Create an incident map associated with the disaster
- Publish the initial report associated with the disaster

Reminder, while this scenario demonstrates the following of a specific disaster
incident, the techniques and procedures can be applied to other incident types
and missions.

The next lesson will explore the COP in greater detail.

Lesson 6: DHS COP Contributor Scenario

Lesson Overview

In the following lesson, a National Operations Center (NOC) analyst will use the DHS COP application to monitor and add new information to an existing suspicious incident and to new incidents as they arise. Additionally, local responders will access the DHS COP through their mobile devices to compare photographs of suspicious packages.

Objectives: At the end of this lesson, the learner will be able to:

- Contribute to the DHS COP application to help with decision-making during a suspicious incident

Monitoring and Contributing to the DHS COP

As suspicious incidents occur, information must be gathered quickly to protect, prevent, and mitigate potential loss of life and property.

The following scenario shows how the DHS COP application provides a national picture of suspicious activities as they arise, so that federal response teams can determine if a threat is an isolated event, or a trend that will affect a wider population.

Suspicious Incidents Scenario: Monitoring and Contributing to the DHS COP

SCENARIO: On Monday, November 16, 7:30 a.m., a security guard discovered a suspicious package with a hand-written threat on the outside. The package was found near the steps of the Georgia Supreme Court. The incident was posted on the DHS COP application.

At 9 a.m., the NOC was notified of additional suspicious packages discovered at the Supreme Courts of Florida and Alabama.

Note: Once the report is updated, the user can publish the report to the COP Table of Contents as an incident.

Suspicious Incidents Scenario: Monitoring and Contributing to the DHS COP - Transcript

In response to the suspicious packages found at the Supreme Courts of Georgia, Florida, and Alabama, the NOC analyst must update the status of the Georgia Supreme Court incident from "Awareness" to "Phase 1 - Guarded." To do this, click on the incident and select Update Incident from the menu. The Update Incident window opens. To update the status of the incident, select the Details tab, and then select "Phase 1- Guarded" from the incident phase drop-down menu. Save the changes, and close the window.

Additionally, the NOC analyst must add new incidents to reflect the suspicious packages found at the Florida and Alabama Supreme Courts. To do this, select the "Create Incident" tab on the Incident tools menu, and type the NOC number, and incident name for the Florida incident. Then, repeat the process for the Alabama incident. Once the new incidents are added, re-load the page to update the Incident List.

Publishing a Media Report to the DHS COP

The NOC Media Monitoring Center monitors reports and postings on social media sites for issues concerning Homeland Security. Social media outlets provide instant feedback and alert capabilities to rapidly changing or newly occurring situations.

Analysts at the NOC Media Monitoring Center summarize the information from media sources to provide a well-rounded operational picture.

NOC analysts relay this critical information to key decision makers by publishing an NOC Media Report to the associated incident in the DHS COP application.

Suspicious Incidents Scenario: Publishing a Media Report

SCENARIO Update: The on-site response team in Georgia finds the suspicious package to be a credible threat, and response guidelines are being followed for an explosive device.

The NOC analyst receives a Media Monitoring Report and publishes it to the DHS COP application.

Suspicious Incidents Scenario: Publishing a Media Report - Transcript

The NOC analyst has received a Media Report from the NOC Media Monitoring Center that summarizes information and provides links from traditional and social media sources. To disseminate this critical information, the analyst publishes the Media Report to the DHS COP by selecting the "Create Report" tab under the "Reporting Tools" menu, selecting "Media Report" from the drop-down menu, and then selecting the associated incident for this Media Report.The Upload Media Report window opens. Complete the fields in this window. The Media Report appears in the Overview window for the associated incident.

Uploading an Image to a DHS COP Incident

The DHS COP application allows users to share visual and text-based resources in real time. This type of information sharing allows response teams to get in front of a potential incident, mitigate damages before they happen, and begin criminal investigations immediately.

Suspicious Incidents Scenario: Upload an Image to the DHS COP

SCENARIO Update: The NOC analyst receives a photograph of the suspicious package taken by a certified bomb technician at the Georgia Supreme Court. The analyst uploads the image to the associated incident in the DHS COP application.

Suspicious Incidents Scenario: Upload an Image to the DHS COP - Transcript

As investigations of the suspicious packages continue, the NOC analyst receives a photograph of the suspicious package in Georgia, taken by a bomb technician. The NOC analyst must upload the image to the Georgia Supreme Court incident report, as it may provide useful information for the Florida and Alabama cases. To do so, select "Manage Images" from the Incident Tools menu, and select the Georgia Supreme Court incident. Next, select "Add

Image," select the file to be uploaded, and then select "Save Changes." The image now appears in the "Manage Images" window for the associated incident.

Next, the analyst needs to associate this image with the incident report. To do so, right-click on the Georgia Supreme Court incident and select "Update Incident." Select the "Images" tab, and select the suspicious package image. A green checkmark appears on the image. Select "View Report" to make sure the image is now associated with the incident report. Then select "Publish Report." Select "OK" on the Publish Successful dialog box, and close the Update Incident window.

Accessing the DHS COP on Mobile Devices

A DHS COP mobile application is available through the DHS Geospatial Information Infrastructure (GII) platform, at https://gii.dhs.gov/gii/home (requires login credentials).

The DHS COP application offers a scalable design for your mobile device that allows users to access the DHS COP remotely.

Lesson Summary

This lesson provided a scenario for a contributor in the initial phase of a potential man-made disaster.

This scenario demonstrated how to:

- Update incident status
- Create new incidents
- Publish a media report
- Upload an image to an incident report
- Access the DHS COP Mobile application

www.ingramcontent.com/pod-product-compliance
Lightning Source LLC
Chambersburg PA
CBHW081852250726
48659CB00008B/2708